THOM PAIN

(based on nothing)

THOM PAIN

(based on nothing)

Will Eno

published with other monologues for theatre

THEATRE COMMUNICATIONS GROUP
NEW YORK
2005

Copyright © 2004 by Will Eno

Thom Pain (based on nothing) is published by Theatre
Communications Group, Inc., 520 Eighth Avenue, 24th Floor, New
York, NY 10018-4156.

All rights reserved. Except for brief passages quoted in newspaper,
magazine, radio or television reviews, no part of this book may be
reproduced in any form or by any means, electronic or mechanical,
including photocopying or recording, or by an information storage
and retrieval system, without permission in writing from the publisher.

Professionals and amateurs are hereby warned that this material,
being fully protected under the Copyright Laws of the United States
of America and all other countries of the Berne and Universal
Copyright Conventions, is subject to a royalty. All rights including,
but not limited to, professional, amateur, recording, motion picture,
recitation, lecturing, public reading, radio and television broadcast-
ing, and the rights of translation into foreign languages are expressly
reserved. Particular emphasis is placed on the question of readings
and all uses of this book by educational institutions, permission for
which must be secured from the author's U.S. representative: Mark
Christian Subias Agency, 331 West 57th Street, #462 NY, NY 10019.
For UK performance rights, contact Joe Phillips, Curtis Brown Ltd,
Haymarket House, 28-29 Haymarket, London SW1Y 4SP.

"Mr. Theatre Comes Home Different" originally appeared in
Post Road Vol. 4, and appears here with gratitude to the editors.

Thom Pain (based on nothing) is published in arrangement with
Oberon Books Ltd., 521 Caledonian Road, London, England N7
9RH.

This publication is made possible in part with public funds from
the New York State Council on the Arts, a State Agency.

TCG books are exclusively distributed to the book trade by
Consortium Book Sales and Distribution, 1045 Westgate Dr., St.
Paul, MN 55114.

A catalogue record for this book is available from the Library of
Congress.

ISBN-13: 978-1-55936-275-7

ISBN-10: 1-55936-275-8

Cover artwork by Scott Fowler

First TCG Edition, March 2005

for Weena Pauly

to Edward Albee and Gordon Lish

Contents

Acknowledgements

With gratitude to the Helen Merrill Foundation, Marian Seldes and the Theater Hall of Fame, the Rude Mechanicals, the Edward F. Albee Foundation, the Medway Foundation, the J.S. Guggenheim Foundation, and the Gate Theatre. And to James Hogan and Oberon Books.

And to Hal Brooks, Julie Anderson and James Urbaniak. And Nina Steiger and the Soho Theatre Company. And Louise Chantal. And Chris Campbell, Jakob Holder, Noy Holland, Michael Kimball, Sam Lipsyte, Sam Michel, Saxon Palmer, Mark Rossier, Joe Sola, and Rainn Wilson.

THOM PAIN
(based on nothing)

Dramatis Personae

THOM PAIN

AUDIENCE

Setting: *Theatre*

Wardrobe: *Plain black suit, white shirt, dark tie. As described within.*

Stage properties: *A match, a watch, a cigarette, a chair, a handkerchief, an envelope containing a letter, eyeglasses, a glass of water.*

Thom Pain was first produced by Soho Theatre Company in association with Chantal Arts + Theatre and Naked Angels (NYC) at the Pleasance Courtyard, Edinburgh on 5 August 2004, before transferring to Soho Theatre, London on 3 September. The personnel were:

THOM PAIN, James Urbaniak

Director, Hal Brooks

Artistic Associate, Julie Anderson

Design Consultant, David Korins

Lighting Designer, Christoph Wagner

On its transfer to DR2 Theatre, New York, on 1 February 2005, *Thom Pain* was produced by Daryl Roth and Bob Boyett with the following personnel:

THOM PAIN, James Urbaniak

Director, Hal Brooks

Artistic Associate, Julie Anderson

Design Consultant, David Korins

Lighting Designer, Mark Barton

General Manager, Adam Hess

THOM PAIN

Enters in darkness, darkness remains. A match is lit, to light a cigarette. It is snuffed out, accidentally, without the cigarette being lit.

How wonderful to see you all.

A second match, the same.

I should quit.

Pause.

We should define some terms here. Then, maybe, you get a little story. So. From the New Century Dictionary of English (*Rustling of paper, in the dark.*):

Quote, "Fear:

1. Any of the discrete parts of the face, as in the eyes or mouth, or eyes.

2. The capital of Lower Meersham, in the north central southeast corner. Pop. 8,000,001, approx.

3. Fear.

4. See three.

5. There is no seven. (*Pause.*) Colloquial. Archaic. A verb. Or noun. Depends." End quote.

(*Rustling of pages. The following lines are said somewhat to himself.*) Hey, look at that. "Felicific. Adjective. Causing or intending to cause happiness." (*Sounding it out.*) Felicific.

Anyway. Now. I guess we begin. Do you like magic? I don't. Enough about me. Let's get to our story. Do you want a story? Do you need to see me to hear me? If so, sorry. Not yet. I'm afraid you'd laugh at my native costume. Promise you won't laugh. I know you won't, friends, I trust you won't. But not because you promised. You'll see me soon enough, I suspect. But not yet.

A flash of light and then lights up. This light cue should only take a split-second: a flash and then a flash. THOM PAIN is wearing a plain black suit, white shirt, dark tie, no socks. As the spotlight comes up, as he begins the lines below, he is cleaning a pair of eyeglasses, holding them up, blowing on them, wiping them on his sleeve.

And yet. Some things are not really ours to decide. The shape of the face, say, or whether we're forgiven or how tall we are. Where to die and when.

Pause.

I'll wait for the laughter to die down.

Pause.

I still sense some laughter.

Pause.

There. Wait. Now. There.

He walks upstage toward the plywood cutout of himself. Regards it.

Oh, me.

Turns to audience.

So. Our story. Don't make it hard on yourselves. Don't be troubled by what you might perceive as obscure, hard, troublous. Just remember the simple human picture before you. This.

Brief pause.

A little boy in a cowboy suit, writing in a puddle with a stick, a dog approaching. Deaf or dumb, the boy is, or, like anyone, a little timid, partly stupid, ashamed, afraid, like us, like you. Our little boy is wearing shorts, shoes, no socks, no cowboy boots. He is there. Dreaming of this real life right here. Picture the boy. A terrible storm has just ended. A cloud, overhead, a little rumble. The boy writes his watery lines. See his eyes. Sympathize with his little clothes. Now, break his arm, give him an injury, some problem with his hip so that he stands funny, can't walk "real good." Now picture that the stick he is writing with is a violin bow. Picture a violin section. Picture every living person as a member of a violin section. We hold the bow above the strings, ready to play. Picture a bird settling on a branch. The violins are on fire. Feel the world inhale. Picture the readiness, the stillness, the virtuosity. Among this, the child. Picture ash blowing across a newly-blue sky. Now go fuck yourselves.

Pause. He takes out a small bag of sunflower seeds and eats some.

Picture, I don't know, a bird. Or the kid, the child. Picture whatever you want. You're free, at least to this little extent, yes? Who knows. Not me.

Brief pause.

You know who I suddenly don't need?

Next line, as if he is asking the audience.

Anyone?

Immediately.

No, I don't know, either. No bother. Or– to employ the popular phrase we use today to express our brainless and simpering tolerance of everything, the breakdown of distinction, our fading national soul– "whatever."

Casually.

I'm like whatever.

Pointedly. As if a grave admission.

I really am like whatever.

Regular voice.

Does it scare you? Being face to face with the modern mind? It should. There is no reason for you not to be afraid. None. Or, I don't know. Shall I save your life? Shall I love you slowly and be true? Shall I stroke your cheek, gently, almost not at all, and bring you a glass of cold water in the restless humid night? Whatever.

Pause.

Meanwhile, we were speaking of the infant, the cowboy-suited child, making his way in the business world. A tale for the ages, a flowery unfolding that will leave you yearning for that old yearning that–.

A man in the audience, seated in the second row, leaves.

Goodbye.

The man is gone.

Au revoir, cunt. Pardon my French.

I'm like him. I strike people as a person who just left. But, our little performance, our little turn, on the themes of fear, boyhood, nature, hate, the nature of performance and vice-versa, the heart of man, of woman, et cetera.

Pause.

You know, you might be better off if you had gone with your heart and left, like our friend, now departed, who just left with his heart. And the rest of his organs. I don't know. This was an aside. Pretend I didn't say it. Don't imagine a pink elephant.

Pause.

Yes, our little story, the little boy in the cowboy suit. Did I say he had a cowboy suit? Not important. Did I say he had a heart and body full of bleeding wonder and love? Not important. Either way, there is our little man, before the puddle, in the quiet after the storm. There is a little thunder but no more rain. Not unimportantly, the sky is all blue

now. Blue skies for Child Harold, whose name is not
Harold. Trees are down, branches everywhere. The boy's
beloved dog jogs toward him, daintily avoiding other yet-to-
be-written-in puddles. She's been making her rounds, pawing
around the bases of trees and sniffing butterflies drying
themselves in the breeze. Ah, the dog. Long story short, boy
loves dog, dog loves boy, no question, no amendment, no
need to revise. The dog came closer, stopped to scratch.
(*Without pausing, he removes some pieces of lint from the arm of
his jacket, as he speaks the next few lines.*) Then she lowered
her head to lap water from a puddle and was electrocuted.
A power line had come down and was lying frayed in the
water. She was thrown some distance, flew like some poorly
thought-out bird. Her eyes were burned open, smoking, the
pads on her paws blistered off. She was dead instantly,
veterinarians and electrical engineers would later agree.
Poor dog. The boy laughed and laughed and wrote
maniacally into his puddle. We don't know why. Trust me,
that this happened, and happened, like this. He went over to
her, knelt down by her. He opened the jaws and tried to put
his ear in the mouth. The dog had white markings above her
paws. He patted it. Oh, the clear blue sky, the whitish backs
of leaves in the breeze, the feeling of the world, renewed but
still the same. The boy yawned. A car came by, slowed,
passed. An everyday moment. The boy swallowed. He lived
through this.

Questions? (*Immediately.*) No?

I have one.

When did your childhood end? How badly did you get hurt,
when you did, when you were this little, when you were this
wee little hurtable thing, nothing but big eyes, a heart, a few
hundred words? Isn't it wonderful how we never recover?
Injuries and wounds, ladies and gents. Slights and abuses,
oh, what a paradise. Living in fear, suiting the hurt to our
need. I'm serious. What a happy life. What a good game.
Who can stand the most, the most life, and still smile, still

grin into the coming night saying more, more, encore, encore, you fuckers, you fates, just give me more of the bloody bloody same. (*Brief pause. Offhandedly.*) Or, I don't know, what do I know?

People ask about the name. "Thom Pain." I don't answer. Or I say, "It's been in the family a while." Or I say, "Child Harold," for no reason. Then one of us walks away.

Anyway, the boy lay down behind the dog, holding her. He closed his own eyes with his fingers. The boy lay in a puddle behind his former dog, whispering, "I do. I do." He came home later, without stick or dog. No one noticed him, the change in him. The boy got some scissors and cut his hair half-off. He drew a simple bone on his stomach with some of his mother's lipstick. He tucked himself badly into bed. He sang a little song without words or tune. He lay there, awake, breathing too much, biting a crayon, trying to hold everything in. The boy smelled of dead wet dog. His legs shook and he wet his bed. (*Brief pause.*) This all being an example of how some days can go, of actual life, of the close relations between man and animal.

Now, imagine a pink elephant. Now, stop.

Pause.

Good. Wait a minute? There. Thank you, sir.

Pause.

Now I think would be a good time for the raffle. I hope you held on to your tickets, on the back of which is a number. We have some very nice prizes.

Brief pause.

All right, are you ready? Okay. Here we go. Who has the luck with him tonight? This'll be fun.

Pause.

There is no raffle. Who said there was going to be a raffle? Other than me? The good news is, you didn't lose. You lost nothing except the time it took to find this out. Which is a pretty big chunk. Someday, some minute, you'll have thirty seconds to live. Think of me, my little comic bit about the raffle. Think of me, fucking around with your life, and try to smile.

Trust me, there are people out there who don't love you. Who don't love you enough to spit on your little hopes so as to leave you all alone, respectfully and truly alone, with your larger ones. Your larger hopes. Which are what? (*Brief pause. To a man in the audience.*) Sir? Care to share your larger hopes with us? (*Immediately.*) No? That's fine. I understand. Don't want to jinx anything. Or have nothing to jinx. Or can't feel hope. Or don't like sharing. Oh, the varieties of experience. Feel free to feel anything. Religious ecstasy, Anarchy, Shivery physical things, Nothing, Blood, Your neighbor, That stranger you married. What possibilities we all have here, ways and means to live and die. Cancer, for example, or depression. Political intrigue, Anxiety, Insecurity, Holes in your knowledge, Spots on your lungs, Total oblivion. More? Financial crisis, Outer space, Inner peace, Shame, Lust, War, Me, Hate, You, Hate, Words, Love, Nothing, More, Migraine, You, God. The things you may be feeling. The list goes on. Then the list ends.

If I were you, I'd be sick of this already. I'd feel restless. I'd feel like eating or urinating. Like going outside and being sick, lying in the grass or dirt and holding myself. Or I'd want to buy a nice flower and stick it to some woman. Or I'd feel sorry. For me. If I were you. I don't know, really. But, again, feel whatever you like. As if you need me to tell you that. It's your life. Yes?

What if you only had one day to live? What would you do? That's easy. You'd be brave and true and reckless. You would love life and people with wild and new abandon. If you only had a day. What if you only had forty years? What would you do? If you're like me, and– no offense, but– you probably are, you wouldn't do anything. It's sad, isn't it? The dead horse of a life we beat, all the wilder, all the harder the deader it gets. On the other hand, there are some nice shops in the area. I bought a candle-holder and a chair, today. I lost the candle-holder somewhere.

Pause.

Now I think would be a good time for the raffle. I hope you held on to your tickets. No, sorry, where was I? I was thinking about your life. Very distracting. Okay. (*Lines spoken quickly, as he seeks to find his place again.*) I bought a candle-holder and a chair today. I lost the candle-holder somewhere. Okay. Sorry. I bought a–. Huh.

Brief pause.

Well, while we're waiting. So, a horse walks into a bar. The bartender says, "Why the long face?" And the horse says, "I'm dying of AIDS. And I guess I feel a little sorry for myself." So the bartender says, "My God, that's awful. I'm so sorry."

Brief pause.

I'm forgetting some part of it. But you get the point, you see the hilarity. It's funny because it's true.

Brief pause.

What a nice crowd. I see no difference, really. In a world filled with difference, sickening disheartening difference, I see none. Between the you and the me. You all seem so wonderful and I seem so wonderful, and so I make no distinction, I see no separation, no unbridgeable distance between us, wonderful us. Or none worth remarking, since the thought of you disgusts me so much. The thought of you doesn't disgust me that much. In fact, you're all so wonderful I'd like to take you home, leave you there, and then go somewhere else. No, seriously. The truth? I don't care either way. That's not true. I do care, either way.

I'm the type of person you might not hear from for sometime, but then, suddenly, one day, bang, you never hear from me again.

We're all roughly this way, yeah? Roughly.

Noting a woman in the audience.

Except you. You're different. You're lovely. I really love your difference, it's so wonderful and lovely and different. Where are you from, I wonder, or, did wonder, about two seconds ago. But now that's over, we're through. Sorry. See you around. You can throw my things away. I would change the locks if I were you. Bye now.

Reality is funny sometimes. Not to me.

Let's talk a little about love.

Pause.

I see. Fine. I'll begin. Do you like magic? I do. It's fairly new, this love of mine, of magic. I made serious inroads into a woman, once, doing card tricks with a deck that only had one card left in it. "Pick a card," I'd say. She would lick her lips, touch herself or me, maybe we'd laugh, maybe not. She wasn't from here. So I had to speak to her in the international language of love: English. To which, she had little to say. We got by pretty well, struggling for clothing and rent, trying to make the best of it, despite every kind of sleeping, eating, and social disorder. Money was an object, I remember, a problem. We had bad shoes and teeth. In our poverty and hardship, we had some laughs– two, possibly three. We had an understanding, unknown to us both. We stayed up late together one night, fell asleep together later. We were pretty compatible, for a while there, what with the dick and the cunt. Anyway, here we are together– eating, sleeping, holding each other. The jargon of romance is almost unbearably precise: "Going steady, Seeing each other, Going out." It takes a serious dose of unsteadiness, vision loss, and a year of staying in, to understand the beauty of those terms, the pain of the words. Anyway, this was us, a couple, partners, un-apart. Whispers like you've never heard.

"You've changed," she said, the night we met. She had watchful eyes, sober sometimes, a natural sort of animal guardedness, a doggy sort of way I found very fetching. Sometimes you meet someone who you know right away is made up of trillions of different cells, and, she was one of these. A quivering thing, a good vocabulary, nice legs, pretty eyes, the backside. Apologies for the dirty language. But it's all dirty language, if you look at it right.

As for our story, if you're lost at all, you're not alone. Don't think I'm somewhere out ahead, somewhere anywhere, with a plan. I'm right here beside you, or hiding behind you, like you, in terrible pain, trying to make sense of my life. I'm just kidding. You probably are alone. Or, I don't know. Where are we exactly, I wonder, in your estimation, in mine.

Earth is always an answer.

We're on planet Earth, a planet in a solar system, one of a trillion solar systems in our galaxy, which is one of a billion galaxies in the Universe. And you think you're pretty special. Math. There's a lot of zeroes out there. What can one man do?

Nothing, really. Or I don't know.

I've been taking vitamin supplements. A– no, yeah– A. B. D. Zinc. Actually, zinc is a mineral. You don't care. C. E. Did I say B? I don't care.

Do me a favor. If you have a home, when you're home, later, avoiding your family, staring at the dog, and they ask you where you've been, please just don't say that you were out somewhere watching someone being clever, watching some smart-mouthed nobody work himself into some dumb-ass frenzy. Please say instead, when you don't say anything because no one asked you, that you saw someone who was trying. I choose the word with care. I'm trying. A trying man. A feeling thing, in a wordy body. Poor Thom's a-trying. Poor Thom is fucking cold. I imagine you people have some experience with the Elizabethans. Some experience with cold. Anyway.

So, the child. No, the woman. Let me linger with my woman a little longer. She still had her tonsils, her appendix, her wisdom teeth, all the useless extra things. This, plus the holes, the holes in her body, in her childhood, the missing things, the blind spots. Altogether, with the pluses and the minuses, a very complete woman. I loved her so much. She had every–. Could I have a little light over here? (*He moves to one side, into darkness. No light comes up. He returns to where he stood before.*) I loved her so much. She had everything. She had fleas, which I think I gave her, and, moles and birthmarks that she came up with on her own. A healthy give and take. We were very close. She felt, wrongly, that she could tell me anything. I think of her in the evenings. Should I hear a plangent honking and raise my eyes to descry in the darkening sky a vee of geese, heading north or south, I take my pulse and remember those–

To the same woman, in the audience, from page 21.

Again, I have to say, I really like your individuality. All kindness and light and loyalty. Or, so I imagine. Maybe you could meet me, later on? After? I don't know where I'll be. Maybe somewhere, down some little alley, kicking pebbles around and changing my mind, so maybe don't bother. Unless you'd like to. We'll get a drink. Should your bright and ladylike ways give way to those of a drunken, cold, and repetitive pig, that's all right, I'll still love you, but not in any way you'd notice. Still, depending on the state of your life and its degradation at your own hands, I could be a good move for you. Maybe I didn't have to say all that.

Again, I don't know. And I may have plans anyway. So forget I said anything. Or imagined you at all. Forget I thought or felt anything.

(*Returning to general audience.*) So, the woman. Of our story. No, let's fuck the woman for a little while, if we could. Let me jump around here. Thanks. Let's get back to the inner child. The crippled kid with the electrocuted dog. Did I say his face was disfigured? Even if I hadn't, can you picture the face of a little boy in your mind, without disfiguring it anyway? Can you picture anything without it getting jumpy and fuzzy? Can you picture even a simple square without it going sidewise and wrong and triangular? (*Pause.*) Like that? I'm not sure you can. Anyway, let's forge ahead, despite our obvious flaws. I'm speaking to the obviously flawed among us.

So, the boy. Becoming a man, in the puddle. Or, no, we're farther along than that.

It's late. He comes home, a dark house. Walks up the stairs, supperless. Something is amiss. Some real thing is amiss. Though who could put a finger on it, in it, who could see it and state it plainly, the trouble in the bone-quiet nights in the tidy house on Garden Street? Having seen the boy, the only-child, make his way from room to room, in search of anything to mother or sister him? I dare say no one. The personality forms in the dark. This is possibly a very good point. The worldview arises at night, without witness. The boy's did, as he grew, changed, away from people, in the bathroom, in the rain, down halls in everyday familial places. I dare say... no I don't. I do know they didn't pat his head. They didn't muss up his hair and say, Good Boy. He comes and goes, untouched, his childhood running out, as he becomes a foreigner, an immigrant to the place where he was born.

To a man in the audience.

I have that same shirt.

Brief pause.

Anyway.

That night, the night of the stormy day that was his dead dog's last, that night he had, with his brutal new haircut, a wet dream, or, nocturnal emission, if you like. Who knows what he dreamt of. Some inscrutably human thing, no doubt. Something out of the vocabulary and wilderness of a little boy at night. Maybe of a woman bending over, eyes open, being nice, knees-deep in muddy water, a rural vulnerable thing, opening herself to the dreamer behind her; or maybe of some fuzzy uneducated version of a girl, saying a word he liked. "Voucher." Or, "Ankles." Whispering one of those funny little words that only refer to words, like "Such." Maybe he just felt some felicific little twinge, a nice little physical feeling in the night, and came, without language. His little bed and the little sheets with airplanes on them are covered in semen and freshly badly-cut hair. What a mysterious scene. And somewhere in the same night another youth bleeds between her legs, wondering what for, sure she's done something wrong, unsure whom to tell. What a mystery. The onset of the breeding years. Growth. The cancers are almost all in place. Nature laughs last, ladies and gentlemen, laughs hardest and best and last, deep into the night, at you. But, think of it all. What a paradise, as I have said. What a surprise to have a body.

Meaning, across the world, hardly anyone sleeps. How could they? Every night spent in the body is a fitful night. Fighting gravity, and losing. Night after fitful night spent fighting everything.

But so that morning, the messy morning of the messy night, that morning on a walk through a meadow, the boy was attacked by bees. A nest had fallen onto the ground and he had kicked it by accident, his eyes shut because of the sun and maybe some other reason he had. Is it clear I love my little subject, and therefore don't pry too hard into his reasons, his empty head, his stupid little agenda on earth?

Anyway, the bees. They swarmed into his eyes and mouth, stung him on every skinny surface. The boy did not, at first, make any sound. The poor thing did not understand. He thought, out in the meadow, that he had done something wrong. He thought that the pain was already in his body and was only coming out then to punish him, that the bees had only happened along later and were trying to help. His body was exploding in painful sores, which the bees were trying to salve, to soothe. This, according to him. He really didn't understand things. Kind of beautiful, if you like that sort of thing. If you like the idea of a little boy desperately spreading stinging bees over his bleeding body. Desperately yelling "Help me, Bees, Help," and putting his little swollen hand into the hive for more.

We've all made similar mistakes. Mistaking the bee for the flower, giving our heart away to the first prick or bitch to come down the trickling river. Anyway, the boy crawled enough away, almost died, lay there until evening, neither crying nor laughing, a thing of nature, in pain among the crickets and frogs.

Pause.

So that's the bee incident.

Pause.

I have an incredibly rich interior life.

A long pause. Even, a minute. THOM PAIN regards the audience. He does nothing.

Yeah.

Brief pause.

You really are very forgiving. To let me get lost like this. No one else lets me do anything. Everyone else always has little tips about my soul, nitpicking about my psyche. "Hey, what about a haircut? Must you be exactly that tall? Maybe you could talk different. Why are you looking east? Don't stand so straight. Is that really how you eat oranges? Brush your teeth. Change. I hate how you breathe." So, comparatively, you really are a nice group. So easygoing, watching so gently. Looking out at you all, I am struck by the sort of–

He fixes on a woman in the audience.

Is that– Sarah? Is it you? I can't believe it.

Almost immediately.

Mary? Anyway, next, I'm going to do this:

He pulls out a handkerchief and blows his nose. A small and discrete amount of blood might appear on the handkerchief. He holds the handkerchief up.

Behold. Consider. Use your head and imagine this is a brain. Or, the mind. There it is, in the skull of a boy still in the womb, battleship gray and growing, folding over on itself, turning, as he kicks his way into the world. Amazing. A little boy learns to crawl, nerves firing, his mind relying on his hands and knees. A less-little boy is introduced to a stranger, is embarrassed, his brain sending blood to his face, his mind telling him, "Look down, little boy. Hurt inside. Be shy." And so on and on. Until an old man sits in a chair, the hearing gone, the eyes gone, the body almost gone– but the brain still going, insisting on itself, making itself heard, causing trouble. There, the brain, the mind, in a chair, in a field, or under stars, in the bright sun of Egypt, Beantown, Whoville, all the while all the while fighting, revising, planning its next defeat. Or a man stands before you, age unimportant, the mouth moving, big things going badly, but a million little things going right– the brain is doing its job. But, the mind, another story. It's a monster. They don't know, the doctors, the distinguished authors. But, oh, the memories up there. Her fine hand on your shoulder, on the steps of a museum. The dog at play, with a caterpillar. Insomnia, nausea, ocean waves. Rain, the taste of mascara, the feeling of night, how the world can sound. Such a feeling life, such sensation, yes? Then pile the words on top. And

watch them seep down. Think of it. The brain and the mind.
All that up there. Married, happily or not. Imagine.

Pause.

Or just think about snot. Imagine that this is a handkerchief.
And that I just blew my nose into it.

*He balls up the handkerchief and, with a magician's flourish, puts it
back in his pocket. Pause.*

To backtrack: you worry, you have anxiety, the blood
vessels constrict, the handkerchief crumples, it's a headache,
a migraine, a blow to the head, and now you try to live. It
all seems so useless, so unusable. The house that you live in,
the oceans, the mountains, the peace-keeping forces. The
restaurants and anniversaries, the factories and gardens,
useless. Fuck it all, kill it and burn it all down, you say, if
you have a little headache.

So maybe I have a little headache. Maybe I was born with a
little headache. Maybe this is all. Just some wrong pressure
somewhere. I'm speaking softly for a reason. I guess because
I hope that you... I don't know.

Pause.

Let's go over the enormous and informative ground we've
covered so far. We were talking– or, I guess I was talking–
about a little girl, a little boy I guess it was, who got stung
by a bee and used to have a dog. Then, about a woman. I
took out a handkerchief, tried to use my imagination on
you. I think that brings us up to now.

Pause.

Okay. Did the raffle, did the joke about the horse. Oh, I
know. Another joke. Why is a fat girl like a tiny
motorcycle? Well, of course, she isn't, she isn't at all. You
should be disgusted with yourself for even for a second
trying to think of how she might be. I'm disgusted with
myself. And this makes me, you know, act out. Lash out.

Long pause. THOM PAIN does nothing.

Or lash in. Depending.

But, to continue. The woman, my darling, from earlier. One fine week, we woke to cold sores tearing through our lips. Picture that we lay in bed: me, confused and not unhappy; her, thinking thoughts I never knew, never will. We were so full of life, each other. Love cankers all. A pun. Thank you. She had beautiful eyes, I'm almost sure. I must have looked. And I bet she smiled, or tried to, through the cracking pain, the dryness I caused in her.

It was more complicated than this, our love. Plus, I lied about all of it. But it was a while back, all some time ago— maybe this morning, or even longer back, early this morning. The old stars twinkle over the scene. No one else in sight. Bony stray dogs roam the street. Stars and dogs circle our house, us asleep in love, or wide awake. One or the other.

It makes you stop and think. These timeless times. How long does everything take? How long did I kiss her, the time I lost track of time, my lips red with life, saying nothing, covering her in me, in my saliva? And how long did our little hero, who I'm getting sick of, lie there in the meadow, drooling, in bed, or, in the park, which we'll get to? Long enough, I should think. Long enough to learn something.

But back to the cold sores. After all my efforts at communication, something had passed between us. Would that I might provoke in you a similar mark, a little growth,

a blemish of real life. Don't think that I think I will. (*To same man in the audience from page 19.*) Any thoughts? Feelings? (*Immediately.*) I'm sure. (*To audience.*) Anyway. The woman and the man, myself. Good good times. Except for my rotten breath, bad leg, acid lack of wit, lifelong mistrust and other mental defects, everything was perfect. Epic romance in the aisles of all-night stores. Unaloneness, at last, the

stupid clouds lift. I have not eaten so well or looked so
kindly on the world. Kissing in the morning, pissing
together in the roomy handicapped bathrooms of now-
forgotten museums. A million little weddings. My life to
this point was mishaps. I was just accidents and wrong roads
before her. But, then, the lost was found. Happiness.
Perfection, with an asterisk. Yes, she found my desire a little
unruly, a little dire, too much of an emergency. But in the
intermingling of our– well, not intermingling, exactly– I
don't know. (*Brief pause.*) We've all probably had the roughly
same experience. Yes? I don't know.

Pause.

So, back to the boy, the little mistake. He's grown into a
bigger mistake. Aching bones from the growth spurts,
furious oily skin, shy to the point of not even really being
there. He watched the parade of life go by. Drew some
faulty conclusions. He said almost nothing. No one ever
asked him what he was thinking, so he never really got into
the habit.

Though it came later, anyway.

I sometimes like to think.

Though this wasn't always the case.

I'm thinking right now. Yeah. I am. We were the perfect
height. Look at me think. We must have been so stunning.
What luck, to be me, then. The dirty nights, the magic days
at the Laundromat. Sharing forks, taking our clothes off,
afraid of nothing, we felt. I disappeared in her and she,
wondering where I went, left. It's not clear what happened,
exactly. So you just try to...

Pause.

Do you like magic? I do. I think. It's fairly ambivalent, this
love of mine.

Pause.

Once a moth was flying around my room. I was afraid. A yucky flapping moth. And me. It all had some effect, I'm sure. Thank you very much. End of rumination.

Now, I'm going to need, not a volunteer, but, a subject, from the audience. Don't raise your hands shouting "Me, Me," though, certainly, I see your point. I'll choose someone. We know who you are. It'd be good if the person were wearing light clothing. If he or she spoke a second language and liked a little violence, that'd be great. So, let's see.

He is looking around, perhaps walking through the audience. The house lights may come up.

I apologize for this, we all hate things like this. But in order for me to fully prove my point, to really ram the thing home, I need a subject. A volunteer, really. One of you watchers. One of you lovely pounding hearts. Now. Who, who, who. Or, whom.

Pause. He continues, while speaking the lines below, to look through the audience for a subject.

I sounded like an owl just then. Anyway. How about this recent weather. You know? What a day to be outside. I saw someone walking eight dogs today. All so pretty, so pedigreed, except for one ugly mutt, a runt, angry and diseased, less loved ergo less loveable. I hope you're paying attention. I am– because of my own pains– going to make someone else suffer, without proportion. Because this is not my dream of her in lazy rivers, because I miss her leg around my neck, someone is going to pay. The leashes were all tangled. I really apologize. But. So. Now. Our volunteer, our conscript. Anyone will do, but it has to be someone. Who of you deserves it most? Who shall join me? I see some of you are game.

Long pause.

You know what– skip it. Thank you, though.

Pause. He looks at his watch.

So life for the little boy, now a little man, sped up and sped up. He was schooled, to no effect, and left home, saying only, "I'm going somewhere else now." His mother wept, due to an unrelated malady. His father, who is still alive, God rest his soul, waved goodbye. And so, our young man, to a city. He got jobs. You may have seen him, something close enough. He's the man waving the flag that says PARKING, next to a sign that says PARKING. He's dressed as a telephone, handing out flyers concerning telephones. He's picking up trash, eating in doorways, eyes down, an expressionless expression. He's just like you, or, is you, or he isn't and doesn't like you. See the former child. Hated by life, about my size, losing weight, working for shit pay, no real belongings other than a dictionary.

One night, picture it a winter night, one night in a park, walking off the day's food poisoning, he came upon some vomit, vomited, and then collapsed. He wondered, as he shivered on the freezing ground, covered in stomach fluid, saliva, and bile, if there might be, you know, more to life than this. Nearby, a brightly-lit skating rink. He lay there, in the slush, listening to Christmas music and chirping elegies to reindeer and snow. The shivers of his childhood came, then went, then returned redoubled and stopped. He got up and went over to the rink, leaned on the side. Families glided by. Couples. Call it the Christmas spirit, call it a coincidence, call it whatever you like, but, suddenly, in the bright light and beautiful music, he got sick and collapsed again.

That next day, at the city morgue, where he was painting the bathrooms, he saw her. He felt light and sick, sad but true, high on the fumes. He watched her cry. She was perfect in her grief. A born widow, or orphan, a person of serious and recent loss. You can guess the rest, so I could leave it at that, but I'll tell you. She didn't see him, never would, and that was the end of that. I probably shouldn't have even mentioned it. But it was a start.

Pause. Looking into audience.

You're a nice-looking crowd. I see we have some couples here tonight. And on came the animals, two by two. (*He nods, "Yes." Earnestly, kindly.*) Good for you. Really, good for you.

Brief pause.

Anyway, a few seasons later, picture him sitting nowhere really, a nice day in terms of weather, reading his dictionary like a novel, scanning ahead to see if the story picks up. Remember, the man is the boy, from earlier. He is not really outfitted for this life, not properly clothed, not enough skin. He reads on, absently picking a scab on the side of his head, staring at the word "demotic." Suddenly, like a beautiful dog at the wrong door, or, no, a gentle snow in the morning, she appeared. She appears.

Pause. THOM PAIN looks briefly off-stage, looks down.

Sometimes you look off somewhere. There's something you want to see. You expect this almost operatic moment to happen in your life, you expect something to appear. And all that's there is what was there before. And you, looking. And what do you do? Maybe there *was* a raffle. Maybe we all won. Or, all lost, together. I'm speaking softly again. Because I want to be heard. Because I want to be gentle. To be, to my own self, untrue.

In a very small gesture, he shakes his head slowly, side-to-side. Pause. Returns his attention to audience.

I continue. Here she comes. The one everyone would agree was the one. Not the widow, not a widow, but close. A modesty, an understanding, a pain, a complication. A human being. Imagine a gazelle, a zebra, a giraffe. Now don't imagine any more animals, and picture a woman. God, if you could see her. Imagine he is not afraid. Imagine he has feelings. Imagine he reaches in his pocket. "Pick a card," he says. "There's only one," she says, demurely, womanlyly.

"Yeah," he says, in customary brevity, but surprising
coherence. Anyone could see. Off they went. To
Laundromats, chapels, and bathrooms, places you've heard
of, been to yourself. The steps of museums. Hand in hand in
hand in hand. She would write him letters, one of which he
would save. Love, period, full stop, probably. Unless you're
very happy or have a good imagination, you can't imagine
how happy they were. They were close. Not fully there. But
close. We hear the word love a lot, throw it around. Less and
less maybe but still a lot. The word love. We mean all sorts
of things. (*Brief pause.*) I don't know. It's really... on this
freezing... how anybody... or we were probably... damn it.
(*Brief pause.*) He couldn't see the story through. He did not
love too much, nor too well, but with too much sweat, shit,
and fear, with too many long words, too many commas.
(*Brief pause.*) It seems. (*Brief pause.*) May every animal find
its animal. Find some food, its fellow animal, a warm rock
and somewhere dark to sleep.

*He is solemn, and, though still restrained, more vulnerable than we
have previously seen.*

Where are we supposed to learn about things? What
happens in the little spurt? In the little time we are, I guess,
given?

*Brief pause. He removes a tattered envelope from his breast pocket,
removes a tattered letter from it.*

Maybe this'll explain.

*He reads the letter to himself. He is further moved. Close to tears,
though still restrained, in control.*

Nope.

*Pause. Recovering, somewhat, but fragile in a way that will remain
until the end. Fragile, that is, in the context of his own severe formality
and reserve. THOM PAIN goes upstage to chair. Brings chair
downstage from upstage.*

I just got this. From back there.

I don't like magic, I'm no good at it, and I don't like it, but I do do a little Disappearing Act. I'll need another volunteer. Seriously, no kidding around, this time. Thank you, may I, you'll do fine, thank you.

THOM PAIN brings a person onstage, who may be an actor planted in the audience. The person should stand onstage next to THOM PAIN, and will remain standing, probably fairly patiently, but expectantly, a little nervous.

The Disappearing Act. Here we go. (*To person onstage.*) Now, close your eyes. You have to completely trust that I'm not going to–. (*He stops himself, pauses, takes a step toward the audience, leaving the person behind him, upstage.*) Do you know, she came back to me, sort of. I had the worst dream, the other night. I'll spare you the details. And the main parts. But when I woke up, I went out for a walk.

I liked the weather. It was nice out, cold, sort of raining. I thought about the world. I liked looking in the dark windows. I just let everything come. Stopped thinking. Let the words run. They came and went, disappeared. Like the things they stood for. I miss her so much. I do, I do. Help me, bees, help. I'm going somewhere else now. My face was so swollen. I lay in a meadow, behind her. I felt spasms. Our last. I like violins. I should have tried more. White markings above the paw. Her pretty ankles, dresses she wore. I lay there. I lay everywhere. Always looking up. She stopped to scratch. She quivered. You only have one day. I couldn't make the matches work. I scratched behind her ear, kissed her lips, her neck. The nest was full of bees. She said I love you. I heard buzzing. My eyes were closed, the sun being bright. I said I love you. And I didn't want to see. I walked around. I left home. Christmas carols played, I could smell my insides. I lay there. Weeping mother, waving father. I sniffed butterflies. I pissed on things. My poor face. I ate scraps. Wanted to be a cowboy. Had food poisoning. He said to me, "Sarah? Mary?" I didn't say anything. I thought I'd get dragged up on stage. I take things out on others. Who am I, now, and what difference does it make? I took her on walks. We ran through nature. We barked at cars. He put his mouth on me, and I, a lady, put my leg around his neck. I cut my hair half-off. He hurt me. She hurt me. I bled in the night. I hurt her. I wasn't anywhere. Then I was in love. Now I'm here.

Pause.

You're being very patient.

To woman in the audience from pages 21 and 23.

We might have had something together. Wouldn't that have been nice. Off go the animals, two by two.

Pause. To general audience.

Love. I was lucky in it, once. Wrote a note saying, "Thank you kindly, leaving now, key is under the doormat." I had my reasons, none of them good. Wanted to leave before I was left. She wanted it that way, or would, soon enough. Maybe. I never understood things. I was too confusing. I did everything in fear. What was I so afraid of? I had promise. I don't have anything anymore.

I do own a dictionary. It's got synonyms in the back. Different names for the same thing, to make life seem more full. It also has foreign phrases. Biographical entries. Things about dead people's lives.

Turning to the person who has been standing onstage.

I thought you would have left by now. What do you want? Not to disappear, I'm sure. Then, what? Shall I love you slowly and be true? Shall I stroke your cheek, gently, almost not at all, and bring you– (*Very loudly.*) Boo! (*Regular voice.*) Sorry. Have my glass of water. Your throat must be getting dry, from all the things you'll never say.

He hands him the glass of water. To audience.

Then there's you. Don't say anything. Don't think anything. Just be yourself. Keep in mind how little time there is, how little time there always was. Then try to be brave. Try to be someone else. Someone better.

Whispering.

Ffff. Ffff. Eeearr. A word without definition. "Fear." Nothing to be afraid of. Beautiful. Right. So the little boy, somewhat hilariously, was never able to– (*Very loudly, a last howl.*) Boo! (*Gentle voice. Calm. To general audience.*) Sorry again. Enough. I have to go. You have to go. Maybe someone is waiting. Please be someone waiting. I'm done with this. Important things will happen, now. I promise. Be stable, be stable, be stable, be stable.

Brief pause. THOM PAIN looks at the person onstage, as if challenging him to act, to respond. THOM PAIN moves a few steps downstage.

I know this wasn't much, but let it be enough. Do. Boo. Isn't it great to be alive?

Blackout.

End.

LADY GREY

(in ever-lower light)

Dramatis Persona

LADY GREY, possibly British

Setting: A theatre
Stage Properties: A chair
Wardrobe: A simple dress

LADY GREY

Lights up on LADY GREY. She regards audience, very still, as if watching a play or, say, in a difficult conversation with a friend, waiting for him to speak. Pause.

You seem nervous, so, why don't I start.

How many are we? (*She quickly counts audience, reckons with figure briefly.*) You looked like fewer people.

Pause.

But, thank you for coming. It doesn't work, my life, without people sitting there, staring, undressing me with their eyes, then undressing themselves, brushing their teeth in their minds and falling asleep, wishing they were dead. So, honestly, thank you.

I'll begin.

'Show-and-tell?' Do we have any familiarity with the term? If not, allow me. Here we go, and I'll go slow– not wanting to leave any of you behind, until such time as I– you know– do. So, Show-and-tell: Tradition of the latter days of the waning years of the North American school system. Child brings object into school, a rock he likes or a photo of herself, is called on by the teacher, moves to the front of the room, stands there shaking and childlike, shows object, discourses on same for a few mumbly minutes, closes disappointingly, having forgotten the important parts, managing not to cry, or to only cry a little, and sits back down. And so forward throughout the North American day, rocks and photos, nothing much, keepsakes and little animals, teeth that fell out, an interesting scar. Occasionally, some overachiever with a bodily organ, his tonsils or appendix, floating in a jar of formaldehyde, proudly held aloft, nothing much to add. 'Thank you very much, please sit back down.' Show-and-tell helps the child apply language to an object, to see if it sticks. Helps the child grow in his

43

ability to convey an inner reality, assuming any of those words applies. Also, gives the tired teacher a day off, nothing to prepare, he or she can sit back like you and watch the stream of little crap, hear the stream of little sentences, the human human *ums* and *ohs* and *I-don't-knows*. All meant to express the dearness of the shown object, a dearness that remains, in most cases, unexpressed. There's something impossible about it. Something soft and accidental. Real. In this simple little structure. That's all.

Brief pause. Regards audience.

Bravo. Let me guess– an 'audience,' right? Or, wait, no– 'friends of the deceased?' 'Family of the victim?' White people in chairs. Cheer up. You're all very beautiful, in a very general way. Smile.

Brief pause.

'Um. Oh. I don't know.'

You do all look so nice. In this very low light.

Now.

Pause.

My childhood was, what should we say, humanistic. Not that anyone asked. But, yes, it gave the impression of a childhood, while it was going by. Like anyone's, I don't doubt. All the bells and whistles, a generally screaming age, skinned knees and girlish pain. I look back on my childhood, in the evenings. I think of things I could have said. I try to picture old things, people's faces, feelings, get drunk on nostalgia, alcohol. Which leaves me my mornings free, to do with as I despise or like. To recover from the wasted night, do dishes, lacerate the woman back into the girl. I try to read or do watercolors, sinking sidewise and deeper into the life we all agree we thought we would avoid. Do I gather from your polite lack of response that we have some kind of understanding? A little sympathy, do I sense in the silence? Or just a polite lack of response. I could never differentiate.

Brief pause.

A girl needs a name, doesn't she. Jennifer should do, Jen. So. Jennifer has brown hair, completely arresting and sparkling dark– you know what, you've seen a girl before. Jennifer is the girl you see when someone says 'girl.' She is walking home from school, as she suddenly appears in our story, thinking about her assignment, show-and-tell tomorrow. She is walking past houses, through wheatfields, men watching her pass, then a wide empty road, a pretty dress, she is girly, the days getting shorter. I see this in a rural sort of setting, autumnal. It could happen anywhere, anytime. But I give you waving wheatfields, blue skies, a girl walking through them, under them. I give you horseflies and falling leaves. (*Very brief pause.*) You're welcome. We see her blink slowly, push her hair behind her ears. I don't know why.

Brief pause.

She is thinking about her life, possibly.

Brief pause.

I like drama.

Longer pause.

You too, I can tell.

Jennifer. A girl, a body, alive in the night and morning. See the girl. You understand what it means to be human. Jen is keeping busy around the house, being human.

There is nothing we need to pretend.

Brief pause.

I caught the acting bug when I was very young. Maybe it was just a rash. The doctors said it was all in my head. Then they said it had spread to my spine. Me and my acting bug, my metal back brace, dreams of treading the boards, eight

years old, unable to walk. It turned out to be something
viral, something you just get. People came by, stared, told
me what I was missing, gave me the homework, filled me in.
It hurt all the time but it hurt differently. A little variety, in
the laming. I couldn't do this. (*She takes two steps.*) I couldn't
even do this. (*She takes one step.*) I could barely do this. (*She
does nothing. Pause. Slight bow.*) Thank you. Needless to say, as
I say it anyway, if someone came by to quote visit, I
couldn't move, I couldn't run away. And so I bore the
attentions of your fellow human beings, on my back in the
afternoons in a dark house.

Brief pause.

Oh, the miracle of walking, of flight, the beauty of running
screaming. And, ah, the miracle of standing still. Be grateful,
movers. Shakers. This too, this mobility, shall pass.

Brief pause.

So there I was, in bed, and younger. I began to see myself as
watchable. It was here, these months, semi-paralyzed and
abed, that I was able, in my pain, to hone a skill for
something or other. It was from in this position that I
learned that the world was something I might lie down for,
holding my nose while it enacted its worldliness on me.
Similar revelations, anyone? Like hardships? Trouble in the
bedroom– shooting pain, shame, paralysis? I'm sure. But
you take the bad with the good, ride out the difference.
You'll have some failures, sure, but then you get sick and
die. It evens out, yes? I continue, ladylike, but unconcerned
with your reply. Which is not to say I don't need you. Just
not really right now.

You could compare me to a summer's day, though this
really wouldn't be necessary. I could be compared to a
winter's night, too, though by whom, and why? I'm like last
Saturday. Cold, cloudy, over. I can't be bothered.

I can be bothered, I lied.

Life is shocking.

Unreadiness is all.

Pause.

Does anyone know what I need someone to do, right now, quickly? No? It's not your fault. That you do not hear what I will not say. But, isn't it? Yes, this is small of me. But so is this: Die, every single one of you, twice. A cancer on all your houses.

I'm sorry.

Anyway, I wouldn't worry. I've cursed people before. It never seems to stick.

Pause.

Jennifer, we hardly know you.

Pause.

Do I seem familiar? I'm looking at you, with something in mind. Can you stand it? Some people can't. Some people run for the hills. When I say hills, I don't think of whatever hills you think of. We can try to overcome that. The fact that we use the same words for things but don't have the same things for the words. We all think our mothers are named Mother. We may try to specify: Mom, Momma, Mommy, Mummy, Maman, Mum, Ma. To make her feel special, less anonymous. She is merely the thing that gets the name. The body that drifted through the word. Like the woman before you. Who is not familiar.

I have nice eyes. Dark and sparkling. It is said. Compelling, up to a point. I think these were the words. What do you think? What can you tell me about you? I ask the question— what's the word— rhetorically.

Pause.

I'm with you in your anger, your disappointment, or, quote, whatever. Are you with me, in mine? Where does it come from, think you? This overriding feeling, this smoldering something. Have you your hunches? As have others before you, who had theirs? Who would, after dismounting, smoke, have their hunches, give their notes on my performance as a woman lying down, put on their shoes and then leave. Others might not have been so– what's the word– as I was. Others might have been even more whatever-the-word-is than I was. I was desperate and confused. I will be again. I don't know. Who knows. You don't.

You're not the first. Or the last.

I've been looked at, sized up, pored over, before.

There was an American– or Canadian, I don't know, one of those grain-producing countries. American, I'm starting to have the feeling. Decent-enough, polite to a fault, also brown hair, seething with rage, hate, average height, promising at tennis. I felt everything with him, for a while. On a scale of 1 to 3– with 3 being only slightly different from 1– he was, I don't know. In the end? Honestly? Just a blue shirt. Some dark sunglasses.

Brief pause.

I loved that shirt. The grown man hiding in it, hunkering down, making his life in it? Never was I to really know. 'Fine,' he'd say, if asked how he was. 'I'm fine,' his mouth would say, him shaking with some untold pain, some resolvable problem, me staring at myself in his sunglasses. Understater. Leaver. Mouse. 'Fine.' He was a clumsy man. My tireless efforts in pointing this out did nothing to make him more graceful. He cried constantly, or said nothing. If he talked he talked about the weather, but he never seemed willing to do anything about it. He would stare at me, blankly, waiting, and I would tell him to stop. He would. Fine. The way I go on, you'd think that I was born with minty fresh breath, that I grew money under my arms. No, I had my imperfections. Sometimes, pouring myself into bed, I missed. Sometimes, I woke up shouting, enraged at him for some deficiency in my dreams, or a creak he made the stairs make. Some nights, while he was clumsily trying to express himself, I had trouble pretending I was asleep. I stormed out of places, left-in-the-night sort of thing. Sometimes, I waited all day to leave in the night. I made the most of the silence he provided, and filled it with gory fantasies of betrayal and hate, scenes in which we punished each other, in which I came out, bloodily, on top. I was pretty ugly, sometimes. Still, I have my charms, my qualities.

Pause. She assumes 'ballet, fourth position.'

I studied dance. (*Brief pause. She returns to a normal stance.*) Then I quit.

I can sing, if you made me. If you– you know– if you put a gun to my head.

Brief pause.

No guns here, tonight, I guess? How very English. Not even some lone drunk with a rusted box-cutter or razor blade in his pocket, to encourage me in my singing career. Well, it's the thought that counts.

Pause. Sings.

'In the jungle, the mighty jungle...'

'Do, a deer, a female deer; re, a drop of golden sun; mi, a name I call myself; fa, a long long way to run.'

Speaks.

Why don't we forget the singing.

Long pause.

I was thinking about something else.

Brief pause.

Does this ever happen to you? (*Brief pause.*) You're looking for something, a word or some old toy. Something by which you will be revealed, expressed. Wondering what the story of yourself is, and, how to tell it. And why. It did, to her. Jen. Rejected items would include: a dead aunt's radio, a dead dog's dog tag, two pieces of glass, and a toy watch. Also, a candle from her baptism, something papery from Japan, an old photo of a man on a horse. All seeming to Joanne– or, Jen, whoever– not-enough-her for her. Her not knowing this is an art of diction and feeling, not objects and props, her not knowing any old thing, a paper clip, a dirty bed sheet, a dog collar, would do just as well as anything else, provided her heart was in it.

There she is, rummaging through her life. A girl versus the world, coming to terms with what is not in it for her. She is all alone. Look close. See another person clearly. It's just me, here. Armed with what? Reassured by what? A chair? Take a moment out of your busy life to admire my simple dress.

Pause.

There are different kinds of silence. You know the distinction. The silence before someone is going to say something. The silence before someone isn't.

She opens her mouth almost imperceptibly, about to speak, stops. Pause.

Which one was that, I wonder. As we continue in this tale. Of life. The sum of forces that resist death. Life: about which we have all heard and read a great deal, I'm sure.

Pause.

Do you want me to take my clothes off?

Immediately.

I thought so.

Pause.

Jennifer is walking to school, through the Americas, the Western Hemisphere, wherever– empty-handed. Long years of family life, time on earth, experience, and, nothing to show. Are birds singing, on a telephone wire? Is there an airplane in the overly blue sky? Is something moving in the bushes? Does she shiver, wishing she were gone? (*Brief pause.*) I don't know, you tell me.

One day, he told me he was leaving forever, and came back with cigarettes. When he said he was going out for cigarettes, I thought I understood, but he came back with flowers and milk. We did laugh, sometimes. I opened up to him somewhat. We tried to tell each other about ourselves. He liked to look at my face. In a crowded park on a sunny day, he said, 'I love you. Watch this,' and turned and walked away. I followed, out of curiosity, hurt, watched him turn corners, double back, saw the second-thoughts, the third-thoughts in his walk, tried keeping up until I lost him or interest and sat down near a fountain.

And so was that, ladies and gentlemen, that?

A minor loss, comparatively. A pretty shirt. People come and go. Mothers die. Hard lessons, in which nothing is learned. Fill in your own blanks.

I'd like to talk about suicide, but, am afraid one or more of you would laugh, yell something mean, try to discourage me from the idea. Of raising such a serious topic, on such a laughable evening. Don't lose hope, maybe later. But, if someone were to yell something hurtful, that would help me really feel it, really help me be 'in the moment,' and that's surely what we all want. A moment, and somebody in it. I don't know. Here I am.

I should stop here.

Brief pause.

And start here.

A girl. Born, of a winter, a mother, crying, and why not?
Was scared. Overcame. Was overcome, and, scared again;
ruined, effectively. Any worse than anyone else? Who
knows. But certainly differently, individually. The things
people do to people. The little years better-never-mentioned.
Or, just, never mentioned. Or hardly. But to continue, rose
again. Tried to stand before her fellow man. Tried and tried.
To find love, in any of its forms, even if only fleeting, even
if not even love. She sang, danced, spoke, stopped. Ailed.
Prayed, for the hell of it. Flailed against her fellow men.
Dabbled in thoughts of the above, grew in her inwardness,
refined her performance of herself as a loveless wretch. Poor
thing, we think, briefly.

I need to sit.

*She sits. Tries three distinct ways of sitting in a chair. Thoughtful
and attentive, first. Relaxed and open, second. As simply and
unexpressively as a person can sit in chair, third.*

I need to stand.

She stands. Posed as if for soliloquy.

How to be, or, not, or, what, because, you try, and get hurt,
and wait in lines, you stand around humming, and for what
for, exactly? And do you want to change, or just leave?
Meaning what? Unknown. Except, more being scared, and
night sweats and day sweats and overthinking everything
and getting whiter all the time, and, didn't we used to be so
enterprising and fine, once, in the mud puddles with the
yellow rubber boots and our little bones and the trees and
everything so full of ribbons and daylight? Before the losses
piled up into a shape as big as we are? I have no idea. What
a life, I guess, what a goddamned life, ours. Very pretty,
really, if you have someone to talk about it with. I suppose.
Don't know. This is just one person's opinion.

Pause.

A butterfly in Massachusetts flaps its wings, and, a whale
dies, off the coast of Iceland. Meanwhile, in Argentina, a
man and woman, hand-not-in-hand, look for somewhere to
eat. Meanwhile, in another city, two people are on a
trampoline, laughing. Or someone is betting on a horse
race. Now the butterfly dies, the whale washes up
somewhere. No connection, or, none known. This is the
world and Jen is at school, rearranging herself in her chair,
thinking about herself, her life, everyone else. Her
classmates, one by one, come forward with some little
something, some hastily arranged half-sentences to describe
it. A girl with old ice skates, a boy with a comic book in
French. Someone with his brother, who is retarded, another
with a photo of her mother on a camel. Jen is thinking of
words she can say.

Brief pause.

Such faces, yours, so tragic around the mouth. Yes, what a
lot of nice white people here tonight.

Note to self: Dear me. I don't know what you want from me.

Brief pause.

I broke my arm in a foreign country once. No language, the
wrong money, couldn't describe the pain, so, no one could
help. I was offered words without vowels, small portions of
uncomforting food. I tried to be still, I shook. An animal at
the veterinarians. As far away as you could get. I don't think
that country's even still a country. And now I stand before
you now. Believing things are different. Yelp. Bark. Growl.
Yawn. Probably Not. Maybe.

Jennifer's teacher says, Jennifer?

Somewhere somewhere else, the blue shirt and sunglasses
are clearing customs, nothing to declare, smiling or crying
or neither, how would I know. Hard to know. When the
person who speaks to your soul doesn't talk to you anymore.
And there you are, left not knowing what to say, stripped of

your previous meanings. Maybe you touch your hair. You don't know what to do. Leaving you like Jennifer, who moves to the front of the room.

And what have you brought in for us, today?, the teacher asks.

This, Jennifer says, holding nothing.

The children sit there, like you, and she takes off her black shoes. It was nice to be held, to not feel alone. She takes off her socks. The children, like you, say nothing. Like my weakling, the town crier, now departed. For my thing, I brought in this, she says, and takes off her dress, her underwear. She is naked before them. He said nice things, sometimes, when he spoke. I thought he was fewer people. This is my arms. This is from where I fell once. The teacher is slowly hyperventilating. These are my little feet, she says, pointing. This is for being a girl. I like running. A pet dog someone brought in barks. Hands slowly go up. Where did you get it, one boy asks. It's mine, she says. Can we touch it, a boy with asthma asks, breathing wrong. Jennifer stands still. He told me I was beautiful. I started thinking I was beautiful. Some of the children cried. I don't have anything. I have a house and some family and people I know and toys and I don't have anything. She stands there. I stand here. Naked and controlling the shaking. Trying to fall in love with breathing. Everyone looking and seeing. I've disappointed you, I can tell, my dress still on. Try to understand. I'm cold. She says. We were quite a pair. Back in the day. It's a big ocean, the Atlantic. Fuck it. To be loved and held. That's all, she says. Love. Keep high watch. Your time is coming. This is all that's left of me. This, she says. Look at lucky you. All so beautiful, so countable, and inconsolable. (*Brief pause.*) Have we lost anyone? (*She quickly scans the audience.*) Of course we have. And all stare straight ahead. As she puts on her clothes and stands there, clothed, hoping they saw her or understood, wanting everything to be different, or over. That's all. And what a lovely ending–

all of us here, no longer waiting, the pretty light leaving all the pretty eyes. Look at you all. Ghost-white with life and your own terrible secret. Live with it and never tell anyone. Good night.

And now to bed. The End, yes?

Lights fade to black, as she begins to undress.

End.

MR. THEATRE COMES
HOME DIFFERENT

Dramatis Persona

MR. THEATRE

Setting: *The stage set of a living room. A table with a telephone and a vase of flowers on it.*

MR. THEATRE

He enters with an open umbrella. He shakes the rain off of it and places it in a stand. He checks his watch, takes his coat off, looks around as if expecting someone. He ponders over the set and, then, he sees the audience. He stares. He stands. He starts to leave and then turns around. He flips the table out of his way, kicks the chairs over.

Strike the set! Strike the world! My former life, gone! Everything stricken, struck, gotten rid of. Now, set the stage again for something nothing less than me: some man, a wound; an animal, with English. Here I am. I am come! Born from the wings, or somewhere in the back of the theatre. Alone. (*He sees the telephone.*) But whom have we here? Someone? (*He picks up the telephone.*) Hello? No one? Prop. (*He throws the telephone aside. He notices a flower on the floor.*) Speaking of nature– which I was, and still am, and always will be– here is some that someone planted here. (*He picks it up.*) Good evening, flower. Did you grow today? Get some sun? Look at you, you lovely fresh cut dying thing. Have you come to upstage me? (*He eats the flower.*) That tasted the way you would think a flower should. (*He chews.*) This last, I find a terribly suggestive remark. But I meant for it to suggest or augur nothing; beyond that of my darker purpose, which is, in fact, dark. Is, in deed, darker. But, between you, me and the lighting, I should tell you, in an aside: whisper, whisper, whisper.

Gentle's none, my name is blank. And I have come and kicked things over. I have breathed badly. I will act quickly, entertain myself, and then leave. This is my character, as I would have you have it; and this, my interior life, as I would, for you, outwardly live it. (*He kicks a chair off stage. Laughing.*) But I– I would like you to know– I yearn.

Witness me yearn.

(*On bended knee.*) My love! my love! if you are out there: why don't you love me, and why aren't you out there? I should look up your old address. So as for us to enact the love scene that is coming. That is here. Now! Kiss my moving mouth. I am all afire, burning. (*He purses his lips as if to kiss, closes his eyes, and rises to stand on the tips of his toes. He stands, so, and then opens his eyes and unpurses his lips.*) By the way, the fire exits are located here and here, and in the event of a fire, or should you hear a fire alarm, or should you see someone run screaming past you in flames, or simply should you panic, anxious, and seek to suffer alone, like an injured thing does, please use the doors, either there or there, and peaceably remove yourself. But not now, stay seated now, for the climax– if I can make it come– is coming. Something climactic is nigh.

Here cometh the storm scene! Shaken by a teenage stagehand from a box up in the flies! Rise! Rain your fake rain and drown the fake world! Make the paint peel and the floorboards buckle! Come sideways, hail, sleet, serious weather, rain! Ruin every wedding and parade! Mess up my hair, make my bones ache! Wrack, weather! Wrack!

But first, stop.

Not so fast.

Here comes the calm. The calm during the storm. Do you hear birds singing? I don't. And it's for me that they're not singing. No explanation is needed. But as for exposition: you should see certain parts of my anatomy. You should see the mess of bed I rise from in the afternoon, looking in a mirror to see the damage done in the night, checking myself for some rare infection and or new sore having come. Making sure– ensuring– that my hair and gums and face are all receding, leaving me left with only eyes left left to stare from. And I stare. Hands in lap, I think of one Easter, one spring; me in a suit, clean; the world sparkling; hunting scenes on the dishes; the feet beneath the table. But enough talk of mirrors and of reflections of what once was but now is no longer.

Where were we? I believe, over here. And in love, wasn't it? It was sweet, wasn't it? But now it's over, is it not? When I'm gone, I'll be gone. I wish the little life I lived tonight were different. Were more lived. But I am glad I ate that flower. Would that the world entire were a flower for me to eat. And would that my faked feelings could make Yours Truly genuine. But the death scene! I almost forgot. Not surprising. But, here, now: the end, at last.

Pretend I am dying. (*He begins to die. He drops to a knee.*) Pretend my life was wasted. (*He dies more.*) That I spent my time in this body on this earth dumbly. (*He stops.*) Pretend you loved me. (*He stands.*) I smell bad, and I am in a hospital. I am your mother. (*He carries the table off-stage. Throughout the remainder of this paragraph he is striking the set.*) Pretend I am your mother; that you loved me when little, that then you then stopped for some time, but have started up again, in time for me to die. Pretend it's hard to look. My eyes and breasts, nothing on my body looks the way it's supposed to look. You mother me. You stand there, pretend, and you mother your mother, who is dying. Or I'm your child, and I cannot breathe, as you stand above me, breathing. Or, I am- pretend- you. Whoever- I am dying. Pretend this: that this is not pretend. Pretend you are sitting there. And that this was good. Pretend I'm crying. That you're crying. And that this is the end. I start to go. I don't look at you. It seems familiar. It seems resolved. (*He picks up his umbrella, holds it as if a cane.*) Pretend that this is over. That it will not go on, interminably, The End. People coming and going. Entering and exiting. Forever. (*He comes downstage.*)

Give yourselves a big hand.

You were lovely.

I die.

WILL ENO

Snow starts to fall. We are in rapture. A bloodhound
crouches near, there, by a freezing river, in a darkening
wood. And your hands are cold. And our happy world is
ended. Pretend.

He shakes umbrella, repeats opening gestures, as lights fade.

End.